◇TELL ME ABOUT◇

AIR, LIGHT & WATER

SERIES EDITOR: JACKIE GAFF

ILLUSTRATED BY CHRIS FORSEY

Kingfisher Books

Series editor: Jackie Gaff
Series designer: Terry Woodley

Author: Mary-Jane Wilkins
Consultant: Terry Jennings
Designer: Patrick Knowells
Illustrator: Chris Forsey
Cover design: Terry Woodley
Editorial assistant: Anne O'Daly

Kingfisher Books, Grisewood & Dempsey Ltd, Elsley House, 24–30 Great Titchfield Street, London W1P 7AD

First published in 1990 by Kingfisher Books
Copyright © Grisewood & Dempsey Ltd 1990

BRITISH LIBRARY CATALOGUING IN PUBLICATION DATA
Gaff, Jackie
   Air, light and water
   1. Air 2. Light 3. Water
   I. Forsey, Chris II. Series
   535.20

ISBN 0 86272 563 1

Phototypeset by Southern Positives and Negatives (SPAN), Lingfield, Surrey.
Printed in Spain.

Contents

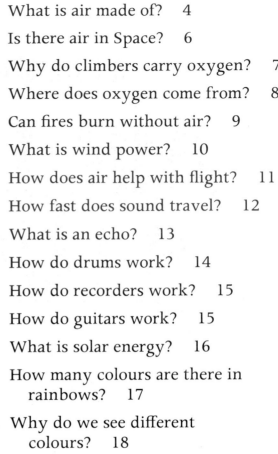

What is air made of?

Air is a mixture of gases which we cannot see, smell or taste. Air is all around us, though – we can feel it as wind.

The three main gases in air are nitrogen, oxygen and carbon dioxide. We need to breathe the oxygen gas to stay alive. In fact, all living things on Earth need oxygen. Without it they would die.

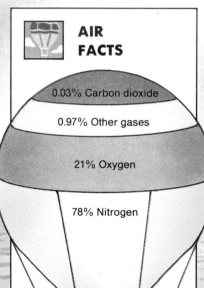

AIR FACTS

0.03% Carbon dioxide

0.97% Other gases

21% Oxygen

78% Nitrogen

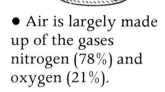

• Air is largely made up of the gases nitrogen (78%) and oxygen (21%).

• Air also contains water in the form of a gas (called water vapour) plus tiny particles of salt, dust and dirt.

Sailing boats and sailboards move because their sails catch moving air, or wind.

Warm air is lighter than cold air, so it rises. Birds can float upwards on rising currents of warm air. These currents are called thermals.

HIDDEN AIR

As well as being all around us, air fills up tiny spaces in all sorts of things. You can see this hidden air by putting different objects underwater and watching air bubbles escape.

1 Push a bottle underwater and let it fill up. Although the bottle looked empty, it was really full of air. As water rushed in, it pushed this air out. That's why you saw bubbles rising through the water.

2 Try some other objects. Push a clay flowerpot under the water. Then try a small amount of soil. Did the flowerpot and the soil have air in them?

3 See whether there is any air in water by leaving a glass of it in a warm place. After an hour or so, you'll see bubbles of air in the water and on the sides of the glass!

Is there air in Space?

There is no air at all in Space, only around the Earth. The layer of air around the Earth is called the atmosphere, and it is about 500 km deep. Scientists divide the atmosphere into four bands – the troposphere (nearest to the Earth), stratosphere, ionosphere and exosphere.

DO YOU KNOW

Compared with the size of the Earth, the atmosphere is about as thick as the skin of a peach.

The atmosphere acts like a barrier, protecting us from the Sun's heat as well as from its harmful rays.

Because there is no air in Space, there is no oxygen for astronauts to breathe. They have to take tanks of oxygen with them when they work outside their spacecraft.

Why do climbers carry oxygen?

The amount of air in the Earth's atmosphere varies – the higher you go, the less there is. People describe this as the air getting thinner. The less air there is, the less oxygen there is for breathing. That's why people who climb very high mountains like Everest or Annapurna usually take tanks of oxygen with them.

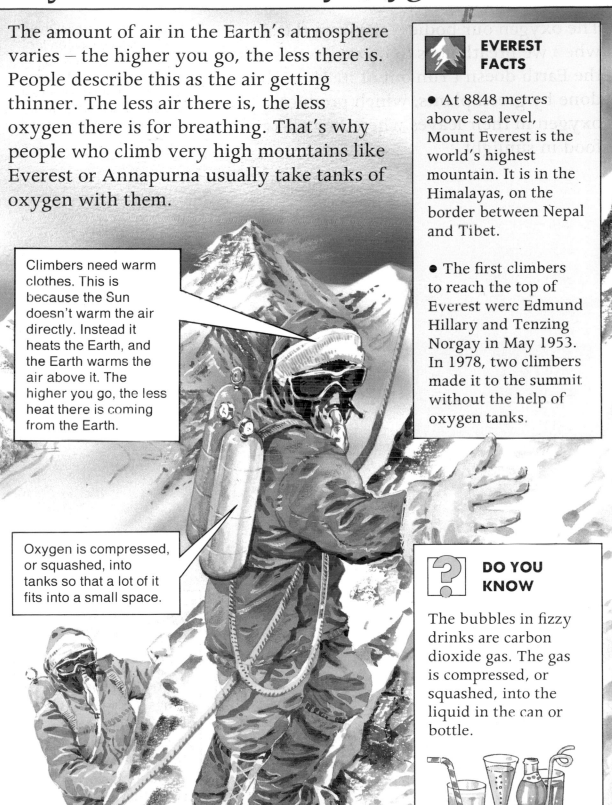

Climbers need warm clothes. This is because the Sun doesn't warm the air directly. Instead it heats the Earth, and the Earth warms the air above it. The higher you go, the less heat there is coming from the Earth.

Oxygen is compressed, or squashed, into tanks so that a lot of it fits into a small space.

EVEREST FACTS

● At 8848 metres above sea level, Mount Everest is the world's highest mountain. It is in the Himalayas, on the border between Nepal and Tibet.

● The first climbers to reach the top of Everest were Edmund Hillary and Tenzing Norgay in May 1953. In 1978, two climbers made it to the summit without the help of oxygen tanks.

DO YOU KNOW

The bubbles in fizzy drinks are carbon dioxide gas. The gas is compressed, or squashed, into the liquid in the can or bottle.

Where does oxygen come from?

The oxygen our bodies take from the air when we breathe has to be replaced, so that the Earth doesn't run out of it. This job is done by green plants, which produce oxygen in their leaves when they make food in sunlight.

If we cut down trees, they can't produce oxygen for us to breathe. Even so, many more are cut down than are planted – a forest the size of a football pitch is destroyed every second.

The green colour of plant leaves and stems is caused by a substance called chlorophyll, which plants need to make their food. Sunlight acts with the chlorophyll in plant leaves to turn carbon dioxide gas from the air and water from the soil into food. At the same time the leaves give out oxygen. This whole process is called photosynthesis.

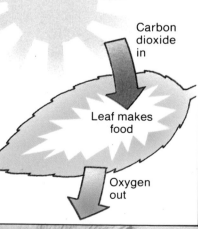

Carbon dioxide in

Leaf makes food

Oxygen out

? DO YOU KNOW

When we breathe in, we take air into our lungs. Oxygen gas from the air then passes into our bodies. We breathe out air containing more of two other gases — carbon dioxide and water vapour.

Can fires burn without air?

Fires use up oxygen from the air as they burn. They can't burn without it, which is why firefighters use water and other substances to put out fires – to try to stop the oxygen in air from reaching the flames. If a fire can't get enough oxygen, it dies.

CANDLE RACE

1 Find out whether fire needs air. Ask an adult to help you light two candles, then cover one with a jar.

2 The covered candle will go out first, when it's used most of the oxygen in the jar.

When fires burn they give out energy – light energy which you can see, and heat energy which you can feel keeping you warm.

MAKE A FIRE EXTINGUISHER

Fire extinguishers work by stopping the oxygen in air from reaching the flames of a fire. Many use carbon dioxide gas, which is heavier than air and doesn't burn.

Here's a way to see how carbon dioxide fire extinguishers work. Ask an adult to help you while you are doing this experiment.

1 Fix a candle to a saucer and light it.

2 Put 1 teaspoon of bicarbonate of soda into a glass and pour in about 15 ml of vinegar. When these substances are mixed, carbon dioxide gas forms.

3 Hold a cardboard tube just above the candle flame. Carefully tip the glass and imagine you are pouring the heavy carbon dioxide gas down the tube. The flame will soon go out, as the carbon dioxide gas pushes the oxygen away from it.

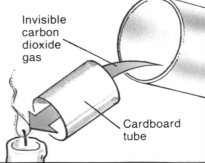

Invisible carbon dioxide gas

Cardboard tube

What is wind power?

Wind is moving air, and people discovered ways of using its power hundreds of years ago. Early windmills ground corn into flour or pumped water from wells – as the wind turned the windmill's sails, they moved machinery inside the mill tower. Nowadays, wind turbines like the ones below are used to make electricity.

DO YOU KNOW

The USA has the most wind turbines in the world. About 15,000 have been built since the early 1980s.

WINDMILL FACTS

● Windmills were being used to grind grain in Asia 2400 years ago. They were introduced to Europe in the 1100s.

● In the Netherlands, windmills have been used to pump water from low-lying land since the 1400s.

● The largest Dutch windmill has sails which measure nearly 30 metres across.

The world's largest wind turbine has blades 122 metres long. It's being built in Oahu, Hawaii.

Some wind turbines have blades that are shaped like the propellers on aircraft. To work well, the blades must be high off the ground and facing into the wind.

How does air help with flight?

Although we can't really feel it, air has pressure, or pushing power. A hang-glider stays airborne because of the way air-pressure works on the curved shape of its wing. The curve makes the air flowing over the wing move faster than the air under it. Because slow-moving air has more pressure than fast-moving air, the air beneath the wing has more push than the air above it. This lifts the hang-glider and helps it to fly.

Birds are helped to glide by air-pressure, in much the same way as hang-gliders are.

The pilot uses a control bar to steer. Pushing it forwards makes the glider climb. Moving it back makes the glider dive.

TEST FLY A WING

1 Hold one end of a piece of thin paper just under your lips. Let the other end curve down, then blow hard over the top of the paper.

2 The paper will lift, just like a hang-glider wing. Blowing over the top of the paper makes the air above it move faster and have less pressure than the air beneath it. The difference in pressure above and below the paper gives lift.

How fast does sound travel?

Sound is energy made when something vibrates, or moves backwards and forwards. The vibrations travel in waves, but they move at different speeds through different materials. At sea level, for example, sound waves travel through air at about 330 metres per second. They move at 4.5 times that speed through water.

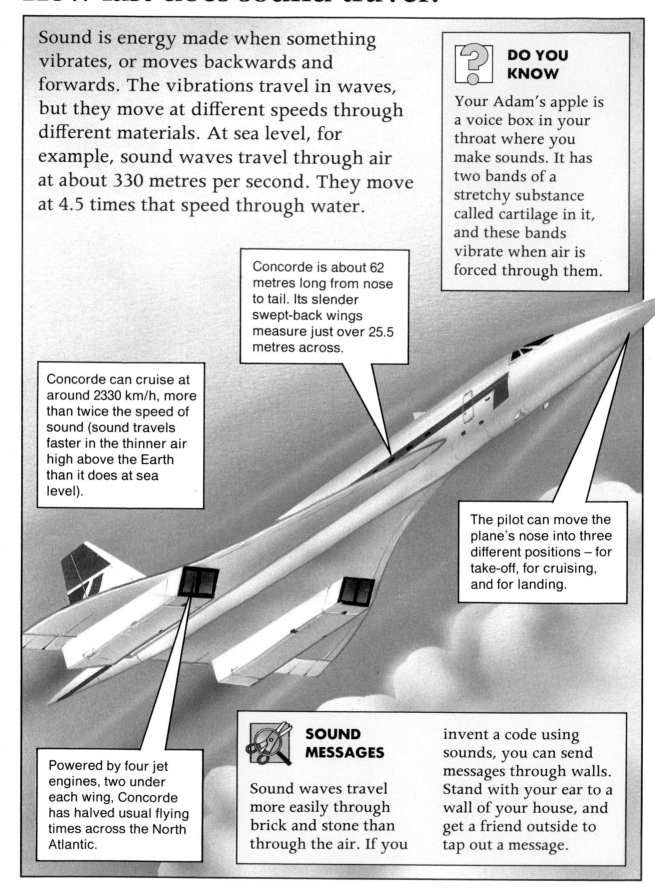

Concorde is about 62 metres long from nose to tail. Its slender swept-back wings measure just over 25.5 metres across.

Concorde can cruise at around 2330 km/h, more than twice the speed of sound (sound travels faster in the thinner air high above the Earth than it does at sea level).

The pilot can move the plane's nose into three different positions – for take-off, for cruising, and for landing.

Powered by four jet engines, two under each wing, Concorde has halved usual flying times across the North Atlantic.

What is an echo?

Echoes are repeated sounds. They happen when sound waves are blocked by a hard surface, such as a mountain side or a cliff face. The waves bounce off and we hear the sound again. Echoes are loudest in enclosed areas such as tunnels, because they bounce backwards and forwards from wall to wall.

Dolphins, porpoises and whales have a special method of finding their way about under water. They send out a stream of very high sounds, and then judge where things are by listening to the echoes the sounds make as they bounce off them. This is called echolocation.

Echoes happen when sound waves bounce back off a hard surface such as a cliff face.

How do drums work?

A drum makes a sound when you hit it because it vibrates and sends out sound waves. Most drums are a tightly stretched sheet of skin or plastic over a hollow container. The hollow body of the drum makes noises louder because it traps the sound waves, making them bounce backwards and forwards inside it.

MAKING DRUMSTICKS

Drummers use different sorts of drumsticks to make a range of sounds. Try this for yourself – make drumsticks with all sorts of ends on them. Try wooden beads, cork, wool, a sponge, and a metal nut. What happens if you use a toothbrush?

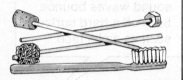

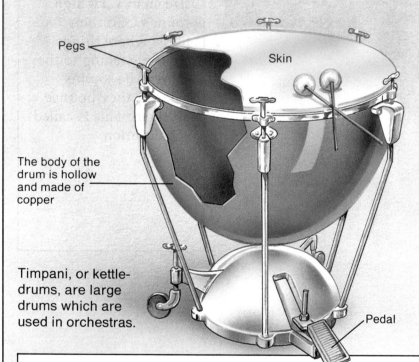

Pegs

Skin

The body of the drum is hollow and made of copper

Timpani, or kettle-drums, are large drums which are used in orchestras.

Pedal

Pressing the pedal, or turning the pegs, tightens the skin. The tighter the skin, the faster it vibrates when it's hit. When the skin vibrates faster, it produces higher notes.

DRUM FACTS

● A tabla is a set of two hand drums from northern India. Each drum has a different tone, or sound.

● Japanese drums are often rested on stands for playing. They are used during special religious services and theatre performances.

● Indonesian drums have skins laced to top and bottom ends. Making the lacing looser or tighter changes the tone of the drum.

How do recorders work?

All musical instruments have a part which vibrates and makes sound waves. When you blow into the mouthpiece of a recorder, you are pushing in a column of air which vibrates inside the recorder's body. Trumpets and flutes work in the same way.

BALLOON MUSIC

Blow up a balloon and hold the neck as shown below. Pull the balloon neck slowly out sideways to make sounds. To make different sounds, try pulling the balloon neck in and out.

How do guitars work?

The vibrating parts of a guitar are its strings. When you pluck the strings, the vibrations travel into the hollow body of the guitar. This acts rather like the hollow part of a drum, to make the sound louder.

Guitar strings can be made tighter or looser by turning these pegs at the top of the neck.

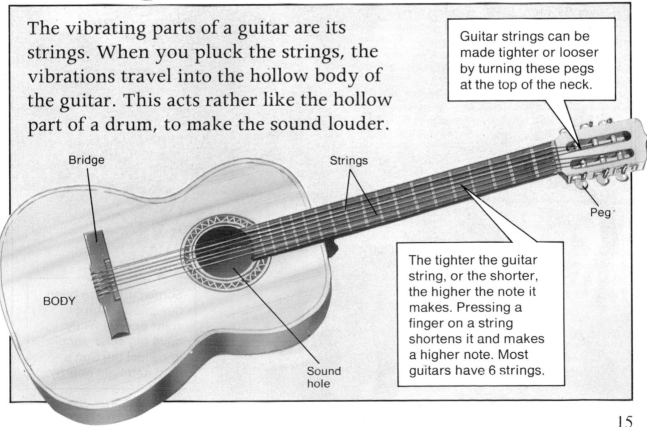

Bridge

Strings

Peg

The tighter the guitar string, or the shorter, the higher the note it makes. Pressing a finger on a string shortens it and makes a higher note. Most guitars have 6 strings.

BODY

Sound hole

What is solar energy?

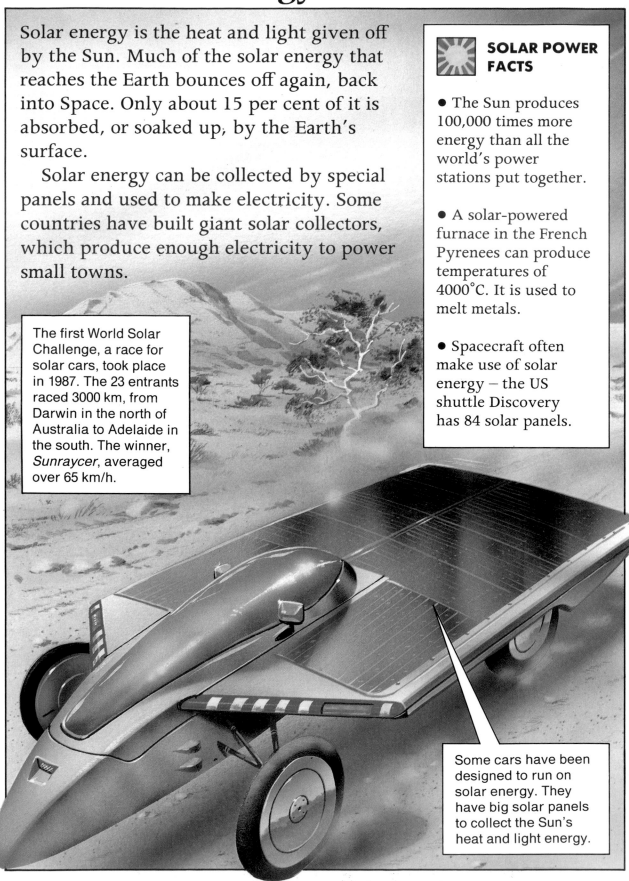

Solar energy is the heat and light given off by the Sun. Much of the solar energy that reaches the Earth bounces off again, back into Space. Only about 15 per cent of it is absorbed, or soaked up, by the Earth's surface.

Solar energy can be collected by special panels and used to make electricity. Some countries have built giant solar collectors, which produce enough electricity to power small towns.

SOLAR POWER FACTS

● The Sun produces 100,000 times more energy than all the world's power stations put together.

● A solar-powered furnace in the French Pyrenees can produce temperatures of 4000°C. It is used to melt metals.

● Spacecraft often make use of solar energy – the US shuttle Discovery has 84 solar panels.

The first World Solar Challenge, a race for solar cars, took place in 1987. The 23 entrants raced 3000 km, from Darwin in the north of Australia to Adelaide in the south. The winner, *Sunraycer*, averaged over 65 km/h.

Some cars have been designed to run on solar energy. They have big solar panels to collect the Sun's heat and light energy.

How many colours are there in rainbows?

Although most people can see seven colours in a rainbow – red, orange, yellow, green, blue, indigo and violet – there are actually more than 100 different shades!

Rainbows form when sunlight passes through drops of water. Sunlight looks colourless and is called white light, but it is really made up of all the colours in a rainbow. The water drops separate white light into all its different colours. The seven main rainbow colours are called the spectrum.

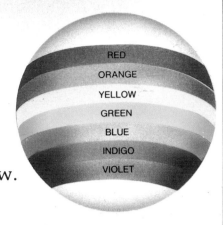

RED
ORANGE
YELLOW
GREEN
BLUE
INDIGO
VIOLET

The water drops in the spray from a garden hose or sprinkler will often make a rainbow on a sunny day. You can also sometimes see the colours of the rainbow in soap bubbles, and in thin patches of oil on a wet road.

SEEING WHITE LIGHT

1 Cut out a circle of stiff white card about 12 cm across. Make a hole in the middle big enough to take a short piece of pencil.

2 Divide the circle into seven equal sections and paint a different rainbow colour in each one.

3 Put the pencil through the hole and fix it with modelling clay. Spin the pencil – the colours seem to combine so that you see white light.

Why do we see different colours?

We see things because light reflects, or bounces, off them into our eyes – that's why it's difficult to see anything in the dark. We see different colours because objects reflect some of the colours of white light and absorb, or soak up, others. Red things reflect red light and absorb most of the other colours in white light, for example.

Things look blue because they reflect blue light. They absorb the other colours of white light.

Things look black because they absorb all of the colours of white light.

COLOUR FACTS

● You can make all the colours of the rainbow by mixing red and green, green and blue, or blue and red light. Combining all three colours creates white light. Red, green and blue are called the primary colours of light.

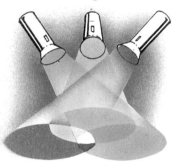

● Paint, ink and crayons are like all other objects – they only reflect the light that falls on them. You can make all the rainbow colours by mixing red and yellow, yellow and blue, or blue and red paint. Red, yellow and blue are the primary colours of paint.

How are shadows made?

Shadows happen when light can't shine through something. Light can't shine through your body, for example, so a shadow forms on the opposite side of it to the light. Things that light can't shine through are called opaque. See-through things like glass are called transparent – light can shine through them and they don't cast strong shadows.

SHADOW PICTURE GAME

Rooster

Rabbit

Donkey

With the help of a friend and a torch, you can make shadow pictures of your own. In a darkened room, hold your hands in the beam of light from the torch. Clasp your hands together and try moving your fingers and thumbs around to make different shapes.

Can light bend?

Light always travels in straight lines – it cannot bend, although sometimes it seems to. However, light travels at different speeds through different materials. It moves faster through air than it does through water, for example. When light changes speed, it alters direction slightly and appears to bend – you can see this if you look at drinking straws in water. This 'bending' of light is called refraction.

 MAGIC MONEY

1 Put a cup on a flat surface and place a coin inside it. Looking at the coin, slowly move the cup away – just to the point where you can't see the coin.

2 Keep still, and ask a friend to pour some water slowly into the cup. You'll suddenly see the coin again, as the water bends the light rays towards your eyes.

Things appear to bend in water because light rays change direction slightly as their speed alters between the air and the water.

1

2

? DO YOU KNOW

Light also alters direction slightly and appears to bend when it passes through glass. You can see this if you hold a pencil behind a thick glass bowl, so that half the pencil is above the bowl and half is below it. The pencil seems to bend at the edge of the bowl. This happens because the light rays are travelling more slowly through the glass bowl than through the air around it, and they change direction slightly as they pass into the glass.

What is a mirage?

On really hot days, you may have seen what look like shimmering pools of water on the road, even though the road is really completely dry! This trick of the light is a mirage. It happens because the air near the ground is hotter than the air above it, and because light travels at different speeds through air of different temperatures. As rays of sunlight pass into the hot air near the road, they are refracted, or 'bent', and look like shimmering pools of water.

In the desert, a shimmering pool of water is often a mirage. It isn't water at all, but an image of the sky caused by light being refracted by warm air near the ground.

Desert travellers see mirages because light rays are refracted upwards as they pass from cool air into warmer air near the ground. This makes distant things appear to be close.

DO YOU KNOW

Mirages happen near the North and South Poles because the air near the sea is colder than the air above it. Light rays change speed and refract downwards as they travel from warmer into cooler air. This brings objects such as ships which are a long way off into view, appearing to be floating in the sky!

How do glasses help people see?

When you see something, it's because light rays bounce off it and travel into your eyes. Each eye has a lens to focus, or sharpen, these light rays and make a clear picture. Because the lenses in some people's eyes don't focus sharply, they wear glasses with lenses in them to correct this.

WATER-DROP LENS

1 Cut a circle about 2 cm in diameter into a piece of thin card. Then stick a piece of clear sticky tape carefully across the hole.

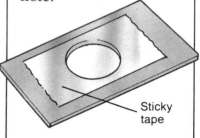

Sticky tape

CONCAVE LENS

Short-sighted people find it difficult to see things which are a long way off. Their glasses have lenses which are thinner in the middle than at the edges. Lenses this shape are called concave and they make things look smaller.

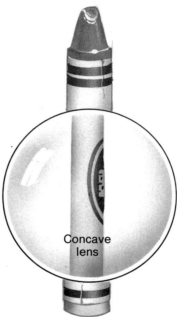

Concave lens

2 Use a straw to put a drop of water on the tape, then look at something through the drop of water.

3 The water makes things look bigger, just like a lens does. If you look at the water drop from the side, you'll see that it is convex – it's fatter in the middle than at the edges.

CONVEX LENS

Long-sighted people have difficulty seeing objects that are near to them. The lenses in their glasses are thicker in the middle than at the edges, and they make things look bigger. Lenses that are shaped like this are called convex.

Convex lens

How do telescopes work?

A simple telescope uses two lenses to make things look closer than they really are. A large lens collects and focuses light rays from something faraway. Then a small lens makes the image larger again, until it can be seen clearly by the person using the telescope. Binoculars work like two small telescopes – one for each eye.

A large lens at the end of the telescope collects and focuses light from faraway objects.

The person using the telescope focuses on the image through a smaller lens called the eyepiece.

NEVER LOOK AT THE SUN

Never look directly at the Sun, especially through a telescope, as its powerful rays will damage your eyes.

DO YOU KNOW

The first telescope was made by Hans Lippershey, a Dutchman who made spectacles, or glasses. In 1608 he discovered that using two lenses to look at a church steeple made it seem much larger and closer.

In 1609, an Italian scientist called Galileo Galilei built the first telescope which was powerful enough to be used for studying the stars and the planets.

How do mirrors work?

Most mirrors are sheets of polished glass with a shiny coating of metal behind them. Light rays travel through the glass, but bounce off the mirror's metal coating because it isn't transparent. A reflection, or repeated image, then forms on the glass. This reflected image is what you see when you look in a mirror.

Not all mirrors are flat. Convex mirrors curve outwards in the middle (like the back of a spoon) and make things look smaller. They reflect a much wider view than a normal mirror because of this. Car mirrors are convex and help drivers to see more of the road behind them.

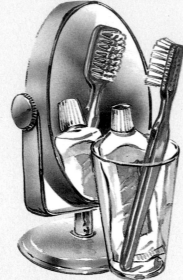

Concave mirrors curve inwards in the middle (like the front of a spoon) and make things look larger. Bathroom mirrors are often concave in shape.

 DO YOU KNOW

Wave at yourself in a mirror using your left hand. Which hand is your reflection waving? Mirrors reverse, or swap, images so that the left side appears to be the right. Mirrors do this to images because of the way light rays bounce off them. The diagram below shows how it happens.

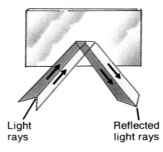

Light rays

Reflected light rays

 SPOON MIRRORS

1 Polish a large spoon with a soft cloth until it's shiny, then hold its back level with your eyes and about 20 cm away. You'll see a small fuzzy image of yourself.

2 Now do the same with the front of the spoon – the image will be upside down!

3 Spoons aren't real mirrors, so they don't make objects bigger and smaller in the same way as concave and convex mirrors do. Like these different mirrors, though, the two sides of a spoon (the back is convex and the front is concave) reflect light rays in opposite ways.

Concave front

Convex back

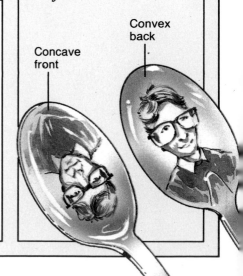

How do fairground mirrors work?

Fairground mirrors stretch and squeeze people into all sorts of funny shapes and sizes. This happens because they are made by mixing different types of mirror. Some parts are convex, and make things look smaller, while others are concave, and make things look bigger. The convex bits squeeze, and the concave bits stretch!

Cats' eyes seem to shine in the dark because the lining of their eyes works rather like a mirror. It's called the tapetum and it reflects light.

MIRROR CODE

Mirrors can help you send secret messages to your friends. Stand a mirror in front of a piece of paper and look in the mirror while you write. On the paper your writing will be upside down and back to front. Send your message to friends, and explain how they can read it using another mirror.

What are X-rays?

X-rays are invisible waves of energy, like sound or light waves. They are very powerful, and they can pass through flesh in much the same way that light travels through glass. Doctors use X-rays to take special photographs of people's insides.

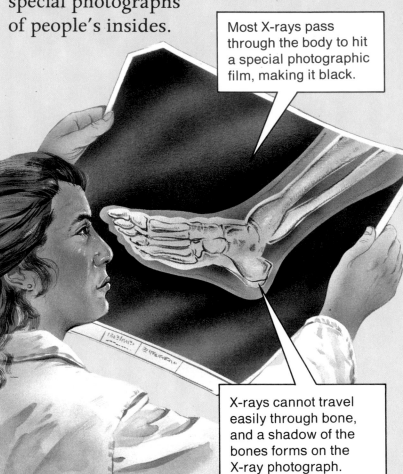

Most X-rays pass through the body to hit a special photographic film, making it black.

X-rays cannot travel easily through bone, and a shadow of the bones forms on the X-ray photograph.

There are many types of energy in the Universe, as the diagram of the electro-magnetic spectrum below shows. The spectrum is arranged according to wave-length (distance between waves) and frequency (number of waves per second). We can only see part of it – visible light.

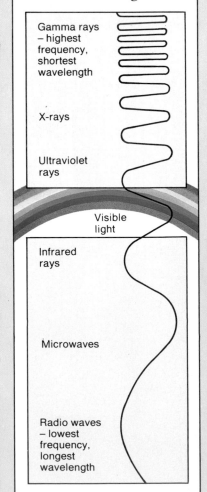

Gamma rays – highest frequency, shortest wavelength

X-rays

Ultraviolet rays

Visible light

Infrared rays

Microwaves

Radio waves – lowest frequency, longest wavelength

X-rays were discovered by accident in 1895, by a German scientist called Wilhelm Röntgen. He called them 'X the unknown' because at first he didn't know what they were. Scientists now know that X-rays are waves of energy, like light waves or radio waves. X-rays can be made in special machines, but they are also produced naturally by stars like the Sun.

What are lasers?

Lasers strengthen light and make it shine in a narrow beam which is very powerful. A laser beam can cut a hole in a thick steel plate in seconds, for example. Low-powered lasers are used by doctors to carry out delicate operations. Lasers are also used in compact disc players and to create colourful lighting effects at concerts and stage shows.

LASER FACTS

● The first laser was built in 1960.

● Dentists sometimes use lasers instead of drills to remove decay from teeth.

● Some lasers are powerful enough to cut through diamonds – these are the hardest known stones in the world!

● Laser beams can be sent along hair-like glass fibres carrying radio, TV or telephone messages.

In factories, lasers are used to cut metals and to weld, or join, them together.

What are holograms?

Holograms are a special type of photograph made with laser light. Normal photographs are two-dimensional – they have width and height. Holograms, on the other hand, have width, height and depth and can be seen from all angles – they are three-dimensional. Holograms don't show the colours of the original object, though. They take their colour from the laser beam, instead.

Where does water go when it boils?

If you boil water in a saucepan or a kettle, it turns into an invisible gas called water vapour. Water boils when it reaches 100°C – it has to be this hot to become a gas. When the hot water vapour hits the cold air outside the kettle, however, it cools and turns back into tiny droplets of water. The steam that comes out of the kettle is like a mini-cloud made of these water droplets.

Steam forms when a kettle boils, because the invisible gas water vapour is cooled by the cold air outside the kettle and turns back into a cloud of tiny water droplets.

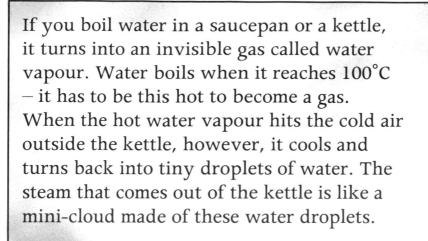

 TURN AIR INTO WATER

Although we can't see it, air has the gas water vapour in it. You'll need a label-free can with a lid to prove this.

1 Polish the can with a cloth, then fill it with ice cubes. Put the lid on and dry the outside of the can.

2 Within minutes, a film of water droplets will appear on the can. This is because the ice makes the can so cold that some of the water vapour in the air around it cools and turns back into water droplets.

 DO YOU KNOW

Water can be a liquid, an invisible gas (water vapour) or a solid – ice is solid water.

What are geysers?

Geysers are scalding hot fountains of steam and water. They happen from time to time, when a deep crack in the ground fills with water, which is then heated by hot rocks deep below the Earth's surface. The water at the bottom of the crack becomes super-hot and turns to gas and steam. This then explodes upwards, pushing the water above it up and out of the crack as well.

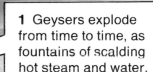

1 Geysers explode from time to time, as fountains of scalding hot steam and water.

2 They form when deep cracks open in the Earth's surface and fill up with water.

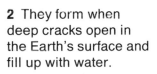

3 Boiling hot rocks deep below the Earth's surface heat the water until it turns into gas and steam.

How do insects walk on water?

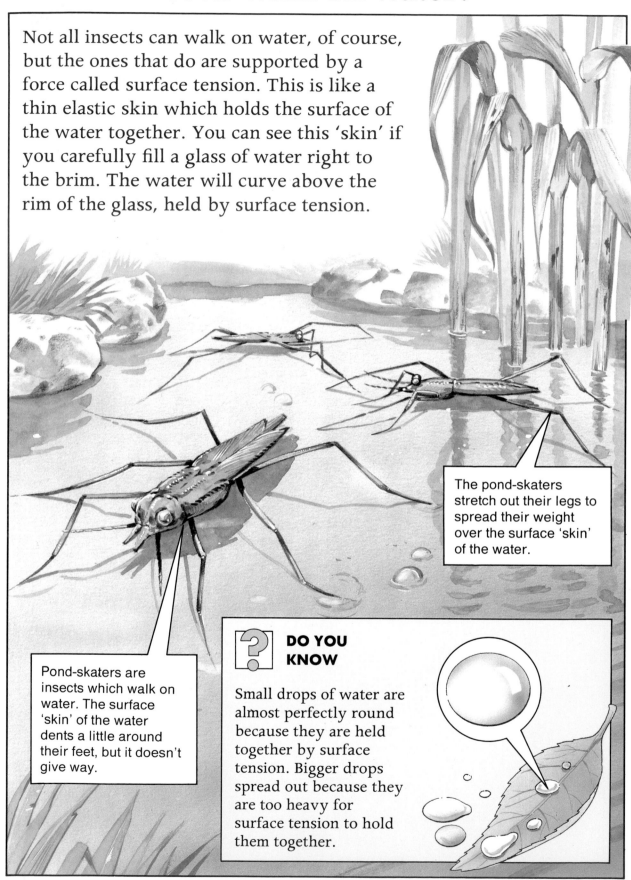

Not all insects can walk on water, of course, but the ones that do are supported by a force called surface tension. This is like a thin elastic skin which holds the surface of the water together. You can see this 'skin' if you carefully fill a glass of water right to the brim. The water will curve above the rim of the glass, held by surface tension.

The pond-skaters stretch out their legs to spread their weight over the surface 'skin' of the water.

Pond-skaters are insects which walk on water. The surface 'skin' of the water dents a little around their feet, but it doesn't give way.

? DO YOU KNOW

Small drops of water are almost perfectly round because they are held together by surface tension. Bigger drops spread out because they are too heavy for surface tension to hold them together.

Why can we blow bubbles?

Adding soap to water weakens its surface tension and makes it even stretchier. If you dip a bubble-blowing wand into ordinary water, only a few water drops will stick to it. But if you dip the wand into soapy water, a glistening skin will form across the head of the wand. When you blow gently into this skin, it will stretch and stretch until it turns into an air-filled bubble and breaks free.

Blowing soapy bubbles will show you just how stretchy the 'skin' on the surface of water can be.

 BLOWING BUBBLES

1 Make a bubble-blowing mixture by putting four tablespoons of soap flakes into four cups of hot water. Let the mixture stand for a day, then stir in a large teaspoonful of white sugar.

2 Bend a piece of thin wire into a wand. Dip this into the soap mixture and blow through it gently.

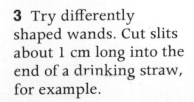

3 Try differently shaped wands. Cut slits about 1 cm long into the end of a drinking straw, for example.

When does water freeze?

Water freezes when it gets too cold to stay liquid. Its freezing point is 0°C, and when it cools to this temperature it turns into solid ice. The gas water vapour also freezes at 0°C – frost and snowflakes are frozen water vapour, in fact.

DO YOU KNOW

Ice-skaters are helped to glide over ice by their own body weight. As this presses the blades of their skates down, a little ice melts beneath them. This creates a thin layer of water which helps to 'oil' the skate blades.

CUTTING ICE

1 See how ice-skates work for yourself. Tie a fork to each end of a piece of thin wire (about 40 cm long).

2 Balance an ice-cube on top of a bottle and hang the wire and forks over it.

Ice-skaters glide on a film of water which forms as their skates press down on the ice.

3 Put the bottle in the fridge. The weight of the forks will make the wire pass through the ice-cube without dividing it in two!

Why do ships float?

Anything will float if the amount of water it displaces, or pushes aside, weighs more than it does. Ships are helped to do this by their shape. You can prove this for yourself with a ball of modelling clay. If you put the clay into a bucket of water it will sink. Now take the clay out, dry it, and shape it into a hollow boat. Put it back into the water – this time it will float!

DO YOU KNOW

Ships can sink if they are overloaded, of course. The amount they can carry depends partly on the type of water they sail in, and the weather. Every big ship has a mark on its side to show how low it can float in different types of water without sinking. This mark is called the Plimsoll Line because it was invented by Samuel Plimsoll in 1876.

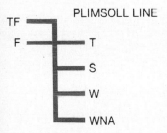

PLIMSOLL LINE

TF
F   T
       S
       W
       WNA

TF = tropical fresh water
F = fresh water
T = tropical seas
S = summer seas
W = winter seas
WNA = winter in North Atlantic

Ships can carry the heaviest loads in the warm fresh water of tropical regions. They can carry much less when sailing across the North Atlantic in cold winter weather.

This large tanker floats because even fully loaded it weighs less than the amount of water it displaces.

Can water flow uphill?

Although water can be forced upwards – in a fountain or a geyser, for example – it normally flows downhill. All the water on the Earth settles at the lowest level it can reach. Some of it collects in lakes, rivers and seas. The rest soaks into the ground.

Water flows downhill because like everything else on Earth it is affected by gravity. This is the pulling force that tries to tug everything towards the centre of the Earth. Gravity keeps our feet on the ground and stops us flying off into Space.

 DO YOU KNOW

When you weigh something, you are measuring the force with which gravity is pulling it down towards the centre of the Earth.

 STRAW MAGIC

Here's a way to amaze your friends by stopping water from flowing downwards.

1 Suck some water up into a straw, and quickly put a finger over the top of it.

2 Hold your hand out, keeping the straw upright – the water will stay in the straw!

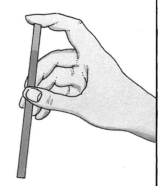

3 What happens when you take your finger off the top of the straw again?

The Niagara Falls are wearing away the land and moving upstream at a rate of about 1 metre a year. They are on the border between Canada and the USA.

How do fountains and hoses work?

Fountains and hoses work because the water in them has pressure, or push, and putting water under pressure makes it flow more quickly. One way of putting water under pressure is to use a special sort of pump to compress, or squash, it. Fire engines have pumps which put water under very high pressure, making it shoot out in a fast-flowing jet.

Firefighting hoses are fixed to pumps on the fire engine. These put water from the hydrant under high pressure.

Hydrants are like taps which lead to water pipes under the street. A hose joins the hydrant to the fire engine's pumps.

Water flows faster and has more power when it's put under high pressure.

What is water power?

People have used the strength and power of moving water for hundreds of years. Water-mills used the power of fast-flowing rivers to turn stones which ground wheat into flour. Nowadays, hydro-electric power stations use the power of falling water to drive machines called generators to make electricity. Even the movement of tides and waves can now be used to drive generators and produce electricity.

 DAM FACTS

● The world's longest dam is the Yacyreta-Apipe Dam in South America. It's 72 km long and 41 metres high.

● The highest dam is the Nurek Dam in the USSR (335 metres high and 602 metres long).

 DO YOU KNOW

Around 3 per cent of the world's electricity is generated by falling water. Water is a renewable source of power – unlike oil, coal and natural gas, it won't run out.

1 Giant sluice gates can be raised or lowered to control the amount of water flowing through them.

2 The dam wall has to be thick and strong, so that it holds back all the water in the reservoir behind it.

Dam wall

3 Water from the reservoir thunders down huge tunnels towards the turbines in the power station.

Power stations can also be built in barriers across estuaries, where rivers meet the sea and are affected by its rising and falling tides.

As the tide rises (1) water flows in through the barrier, driving turbines to make electricity. Sluice gates trap the water behind the barrier at high tide.

When the tide drops (2) the sluice gates are opened, letting the water flow back through the turbines.

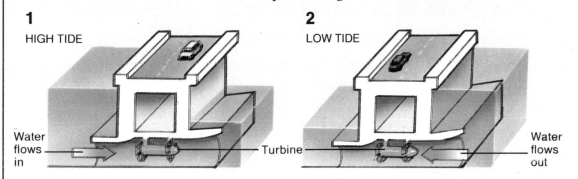

1

HIGH TIDE

Water flows in

Turbine

2

LOW TIDE

Water flows out

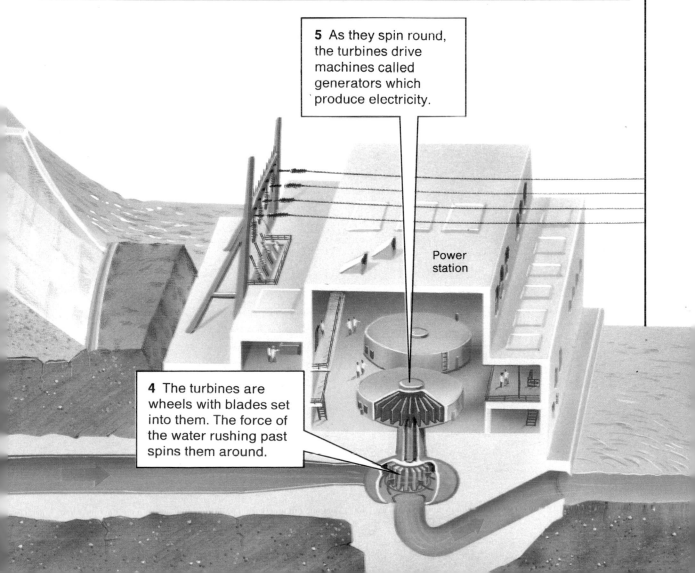

5 As they spin round, the turbines drive machines called generators which produce electricity.

Power station

4 The turbines are wheels with blades set into them. The force of the water rushing past spins them around.

What is acid rain?

Acid rain is a poison which is polluting, or dirtying, the land and the water on Earth. When coal, oil and natural gas are burnt, gases containing sulphur and nitrogen are given off. These gases combine with the moisture in the air to make acid rain or snow. When this falls on the land, it enters the soil and harms the growth of plants. Acid rain is also poisoning lakes, killing the plants and animals that live in them.

Coal, oil and natural gas are burnt as fuel in factories and power stations, as well as in homes. This produces the gases that make acid rain.

ACID RAIN FACTS

● Acid rain can be 1000 times as acidic, or sour, as normal rain. It is carried across countries and between continents by wind.

● The effect of acid rain on lakes and rivers was first noticed in Sweden, where around 10% of lakes no longer have live fish in them.

Useful words

Atmosphere   The air that surrounds the Earth in a layer about 500 km deep. It is largely made up of the gases nitrogen and oxygen, but it also has small amounts of water vapour and other gases in it, as well as salt, dust and dirt.

Carbon dioxide   One of the gases in the atmosphere – about 0.03% of the air is carbon dioxide gas. Plants use carbon dioxide to help make their food.

Compress   To squeeze or squash something into a small space.

Concave   Curved inwards – a concave lens is thinner in the middle than at the edges.

Convex   Curved outwards – a convex lens is fatter in the middle than at the edges.

Energy   Power which is being sent out – the Sun gives out heat and light energy, for example.

Lens   Lenses are used to make things look bigger or smaller. They are usually made of a transparent substance such as glass or plastic. Each of your eyes has a lens in it which is made of a material called protein.

Opaque   Something which won't let light through, and which we can't see through.

Oxygen   About 21% of the air is made up of this gas. Humans and all other animals on Earth need to take or breathe oxygen into their bodies in order to live. It passes into our blood and, with the food we eat, gives us energy to live and grow.

Pollution   The dirtying of air, water or the soil.

Pressure   Another word for push. Air and water both have pressure, although we can't usually feel it.

Reflect   To bounce off or throw back – when sound waves bounce off a hard cliff face, for example, or rays of light bounce off something opaque.

Refraction   The change in speed and direction of light rays at the point where two different substances (such as air and water) meet, and where light appears to bend. Refraction happens because light travels at different speeds through different materials.

Surface tension   The thin stretchy 'skin' on water and other liquids.

Transparent   Something which is see-through.

Vibrate   To shake, or move backwards and forwards.

Water vapour   The invisible gas which water turns into when it is heated to a temperature of 100°C.

Index